W9-ASK-653

WAVES

HERBERT S. ZIM

illustrated by RENÉ MARTIN

William Morrow & Company   New York 1967

The author thanks Dr. Bernard D. Zetler and his colleagues at the Institute of Oceanography, Environmental Science Services Administration, for reviewing the manuscript and art; and Raymond Wilcove of the Coast and Geodetic Survey, for resource materials.

J
551.4
Z

Copyright © 1967 by Herbert S. Zim
All rights reserved. No part of this book may be reproduced or utilized in any form or by any means, electronic or mechanical, including photocopying, recording or by any information storage and retrieval system, without permission in writing from the Publisher. Inquiries should be addressed to William Morrow and Company, Inc., 425 Park Avenue South, New York, N.Y. 10016
Published simultaneously in Canada by George J. McLeod Limited, Toronto.
Printed in the United States of America.
Library of Congress Catalog Card Number 67-21734

All that we know about the world, and the whole universe for that matter, is due to waves. Sounds are one kind of wave. When sound waves strike your ear, you hear voices, music, street noises, and other familiar sounds.

Because of light waves you can read this book, see your friends, and even tell what distant stars are made of. Light waves reveal the color and beauty of the world around us.

Longer waves bring us radio and television. Most electricity flows in waves. A 60-cycle current has 60 waves a second. Other types of shorter waves are often called rays. Best known are X rays, cosmic rays, and ultraviolet rays.

58486

Most familiar of all the many kinds of waves are ocean waves. People have watched ocean waves for thousands of years. They are fun to feel as well as see, though sometimes they become large and dangerous.

Waves make up a small part of the oceans, whose average depth is over two miles. They are found only at the surface and a bit below. But the surface of the seas covers nearly three quarters of the earth. Many people travel, work, and have fun on it.

|← — — — — — — — — — _wavelength

All waves, from the tiniest light waves to the great storm waves of the sea, have several features in common. First, they have height. The highest part of a wave is its crest; the lowest part is its trough. A wave's height is measured from crest to trough.

Waves also have length—the distance from one crest to the next. This distance is called a wavelength. The wavelength of light is so short that several billion waves are needed to make an inch. Average ocean waves are 150 to 300 feet long, and those in storms may be twice as long or even longer.

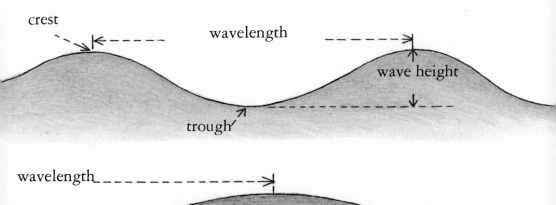

Time for a wave to pass is its period.

Finally, all waves move—although at very different speeds. Light waves are the fastest by far. Ocean waves usually move at 20 to 40 miles an hour or more, and certain kinds can travel as fast as a jet plane. The time one wave takes to pass a reference mark is called the period of the wave.

You know from your own experience that pushing water in a bathtub makes waves. The great pusher on the ocean is the force of the wind. When it blows, waves begin to form and move across mile after mile of the ocean's surface, usually in a changing pattern. As winds

shift and waves come from several directions,
the patterns change. When the waves reach
shallow water, the pattern changes again. Then,
as they break upon the beach, the speed and
shape of waves change once more.

wave pattern in a rough sea

From a ship at sea, we see waves coming along one after another. They are not all the same size, and their pattern may change as you watch. The waves you see may be caused by winds from several storms hundreds of miles away, blowing with different force in somewhat different directions. So the fact that the waves of the open ocean are mixed up and difficult to study is not surprising.

Wave patterns at sea are often mixed.

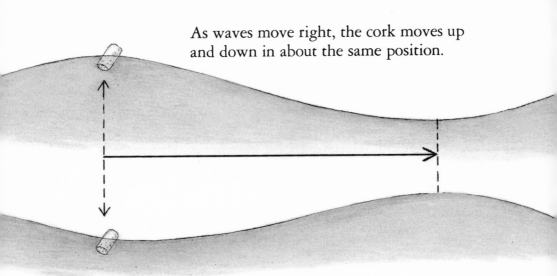

As waves move right, the cork moves up and down in about the same position.

In quiet water, where waves are small, one can see what is happening more easily. But even there our eyes deceive us. We feel the whole ocean must be moving along with the waves. Drop a cork or a stick in the water, however. Watch it bob up and down as each wave passes, and note that it stays in just about the same place. The waves move forward, but not the stick and the water.

Waves have been observed for thousands of years, but not till the early 1800's did scientists become curious and begin to experiment with them. They built large glass tanks with a pusher at one end to make waves. To the water they added bits of material just as heavy as water—too light to sink and too heavy to float. Thus they were able to see how the water moved as each wave passed.

an early type of wave machine

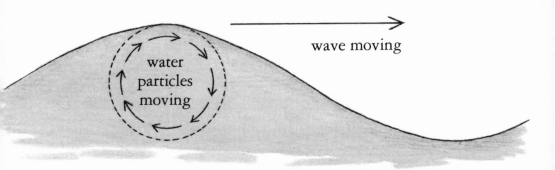

The watchers quickly discovered that the particles moved in a circle with each passing wave. So each bit of water in the wave moved in a circle also. Measurements showed that the height of the circle was the same as the height of the wave.

Scientists built larger and better wave tanks, and soon they knew a good deal more about waves—although not everything. Today scientists can make eight-foot waves in great modern tanks, but sooner or later they need to return to the sea to continue their study. There is still much to be learned.

Research in tanks and at sea gives a picture of how waves form and grow. When the water surface is calm, even a slight breeze forms ripples. Ripples are the smallest waves, having a period of less than a second between one crest and the next.

As soon as water has been ruffled, the wind has a surface against which to push. The size of waves builds up if the wind blows hard and steady. As the wind increases, the wave surface against which it pushes becomes steeper and the waves rise higher and higher.

Three things determine how waves form and grow: the force of the wind, the time the wind blows, and the amount of open sea over which

shape of a typical open-sea wave

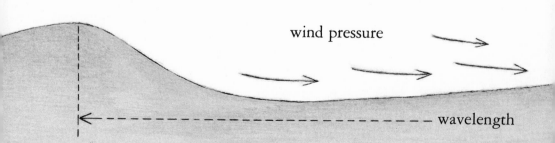

wind pressure

wavelength

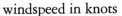

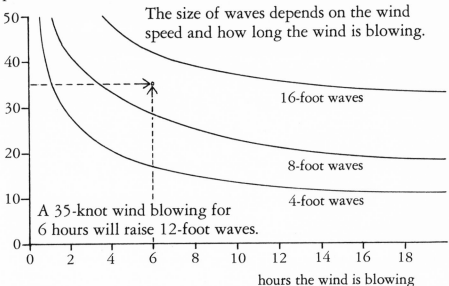

The size of waves depends on the wind speed and how long the wind is blowing.

16-foot waves

8-foot waves

4-foot waves

A 35-knot wind blowing for 6 hours will raise 12-foot waves.

hours the wind is blowing

the wind can blow. Swells in the Pacific Ocean are larger than those of the Atlantic because they can build up over a greater distance. As long as the wind is moving faster than the waves, waves will grow and will absorb the wind's energy. As waves become higher their energy increases. If waves double in height, their energy increases four times.

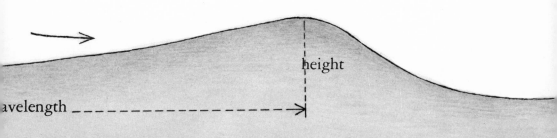

On the open sea, ripples change into waves and waves line up in swells. Swells are wave groups of about the same size, moving together. Even if the wind shifts or drops, swells still travel hundreds or even thousands of miles. They lose very little of the energy they have picked up from the winds.

If winds continue, waves build up into longer, larger swells, as they absorb wind energy and grow. These wave groups, however, travel forward at only half the speed of each single wave. Low waves continually form at the back of the group and move forward into the group. Since each wave travels faster than the entire group, it moves through the group,

whitecaps on a choppy sea—20-mile wind

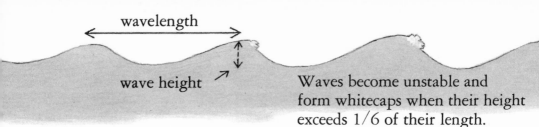

wavelength

wave height

Waves become unstable and form whitecaps when their height exceeds 1/6 of their length.

dying down as it passes out the front. A typical ocean swell has a period of about 12 to 16 seconds; a wavelength of 700 to 1400 feet, and a speed that averages 40 to 60 miles an hour.

As winds increase, waves usually build up till they reach about one foot in height to every six feet in length. As they near this height the tops become unstable. They break and tumble over, forming whitecaps. Whitecaps may appear on small waves or large as long as the wind whips the waves higher than one sixth of their wavelength.

whitecaps on a stormy sea—50-mile gale

Judging the height of a wave is not easy, especially during a storm when the waves are largest. Then a ship often tilts one way or another. White water or spray dashes far above the actual wave. Most estimates of wave size are too high. Not even sailors can judge the height of a wave accurately, unless they are experienced and can see the wave against the horizon.

When a ship plunges forward waves look much higher and larger.

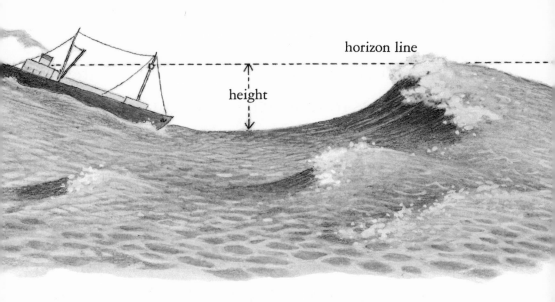

horizon line

height

Storm waves on the open sea may rise as high as 50 or sometimes 70 feet. Waves this big have been seen a number of times, when conditions were good for checking their height. Record waves form in the Pacific, where heights of over 100 feet have been reported. After a heavy storm in 1933 one wave was estimated as at least 112 feet high. An officer on a ship's bridge measured the period of this wave with a stopwatch. He made and recorded careful observations from which the height of the wave was computed.

Waves change when they reach shallow water, which does not mean at the beach. Shallow water is the depth where the bottom begins to have an effect on the wave, that is, a depth of about half the wavelength. For short waves, shallow water may be only a few feet. Big storm waves begin to touch bottom at depths of 500 or 600 feet.

Friction on the bottom changes waves when they enter water where the depth is less than half the wavelength.

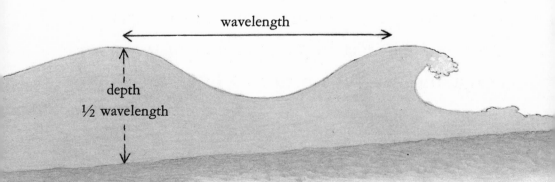

wavelength

depth
½ wavelength

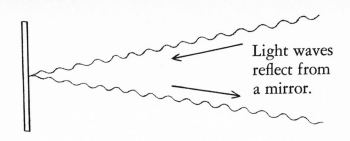

Light waves
reflect from
a mirror.

In shallow water, ocean waves behave like light waves, which are billions of times smaller. For example, light waves can be reflected by a mirror. Ocean waves, before they break, can be reflected easily by a sea cliff or by a breakwater. Their energy is sent seaward again. Breakwaters are built in deep water to protect ships in the harbor by reflecting waves back to the sea before they break.

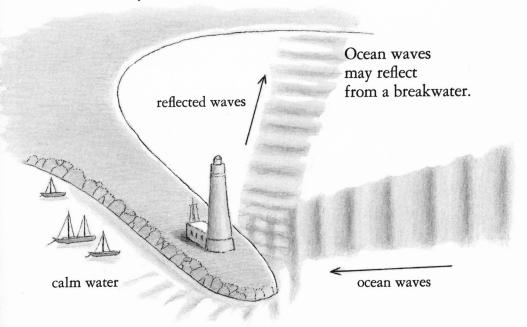

reflected waves

Ocean waves
may reflect
from a breakwater.

calm water

ocean waves

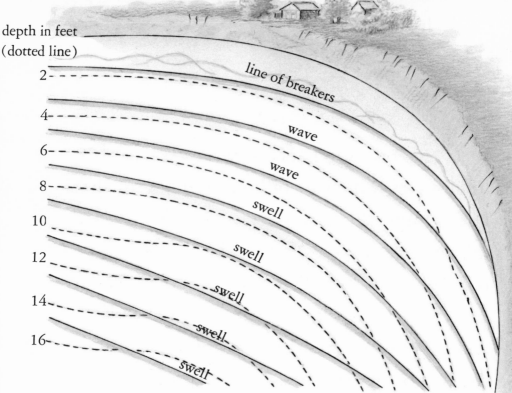

depth in feet
(dotted line)

2

line of breakers

4

wave

6

wave

8

swell

10

swell

12

swell

14

swell

16

swell

swell

Wave refraction bends waves parallel to a beach.

As waves pass a tip of land, move around an island, or touch bottom, they are bent, or refracted, in about the same way that light is bent when it passes through a camera lens. When bent by the sea bottom, waves turn so that their leading edge is parallel to the shore while their direction is straight toward it. Wave action is stronger at points of land that stick out into the sea, and so headlands are worn down faster. Sometimes the shape of the bottom will affect long waves more than short ones. It may concentrate storm waves in a harbor where they can cause great damage to docks and ships.

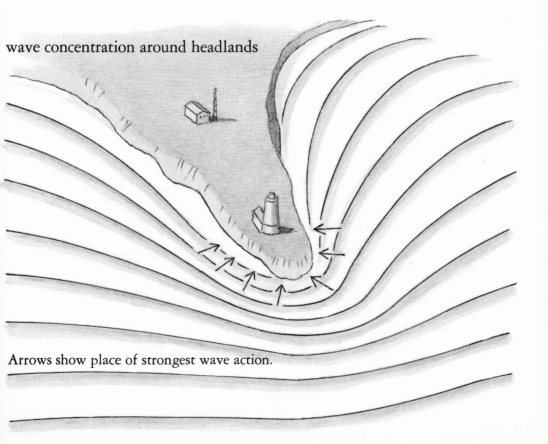

wave concentration around headlands

Arrows show place of strongest wave action.

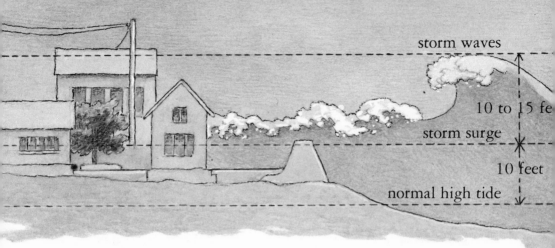

storm waves

10 to 15 fe[et]

storm surge

10 feet

normal high tide

In shallow water, great storms like hurricanes may push water inland—as a huge surge with storm waves riding on top of it—faster than the water can return to sea. A surge of 10 or 15 feet, with waves equally high, may wipe out entire cities. This kind of disaster happened to Galveston, Texas, in 1900.

The waves that interest people most are those that break on the beach. As the water gets very shallow, waves change rapidly and break with a roar. A line of breakers is an exciting sight, for it shows clearly the tremendous energy of the sea.

The waves that come in on the beach are not often the same size. Some may be twice as high as others. Large and small waves appear in a regular pattern; a group of small waves are followed by a group of large ones. The smaller waves enlarge, and, after a point, the large waves begin to shrink till the cycle repeats. Between one group of small waves and another a dozen or more waves may break.

waves of different lengths from different directions

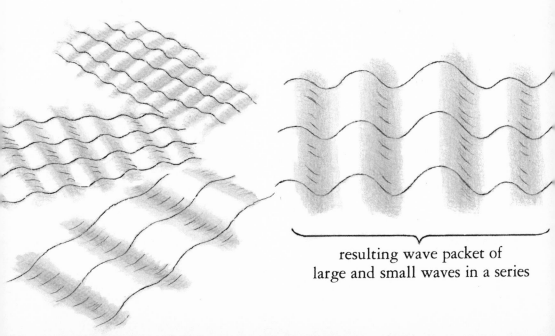

resulting wave packet of
large and small waves in a series

These wave packets, consisting of waves
large and small formed by different winds over
different parts of the ocean, approach the
beach together. Their pattern depends on how
the waves from these different sources meet.
If the crests of two waves join near the beach,
the added water makes the breaking wave
pile higher. But if the crest of one wave hits

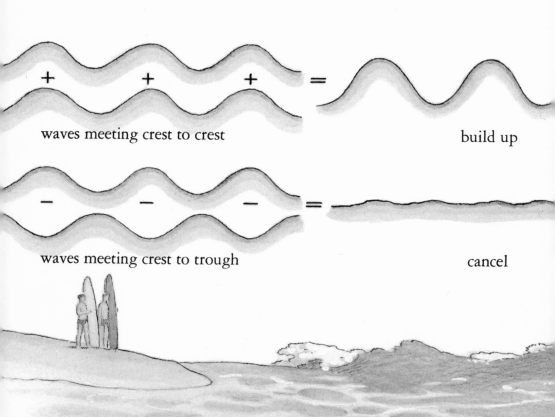

waves meeting crest to crest   build up

waves meeting crest to trough   cancel the trough of another, the waves level out, and there is a smaller wave or no wave at all.

The crests and troughs of different size from different waves join in different ways. The exact pattern of breaking waves depends on wave height, wave length, and wave motion.

If the day is reasonably calm, a person watching the waves for five minutes or so can soon estimate how often the largest waves will appear. The intervals between them may last 2 to 3 minutes or every 10 to 12 waves. If you are swimming or surfing, take advantage of the bigger waves that come along regularly.

Just as judging the height of waves at sea is hard, the height of breakers on the beach can be misleading also. To estimate their size, move back on the beach until you line up the crest of the breaking wave with the horizon. Then the height of your eye is level with the top of the wave. Determine the bottom of the wave by the level of the returning surf. Use your own height as a guide, and you can estimate the wave's height quickly.

When you swim or float out beyond the breakers, you pick up the same movement as

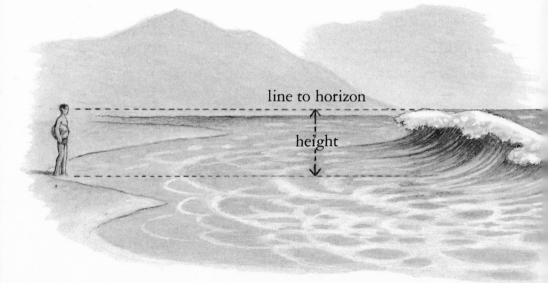

line to horizon

height

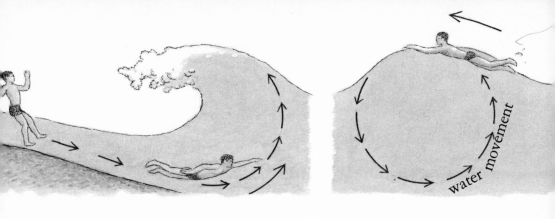

that of the water particles. You, too, move
in a circle, going forward and up as the crest
passes, then seaward and down into the
trough. The closer you are to the breaking
wave the more you will feel this movement.
If you catch the curling crest of a breaker, it
will throw you downward and forward toward
the beach. If you dive into one, it will pull
you under and upward behind it.

The foaming surf that dashes up on the
shore may flow quickly back, if the beach is
steep or the waves large. This seaward flow
of water may be strong enough to upset a
person standing deep in the surf.

All the water in the surf moves back to the sea again. Part of this movement is sometimes called an undertow. When an offshore sandbar blocks the return of water, channels may be cut through it. Strong rip currents that can carry a swimmer out to sea run in these channels. Rips often have a choppy look, and breakers may not form in them.

As swells move into shallow water, contact with the bottom slows down the orbiting wave particles. This drag shortens the length of the wave and increases its height. When

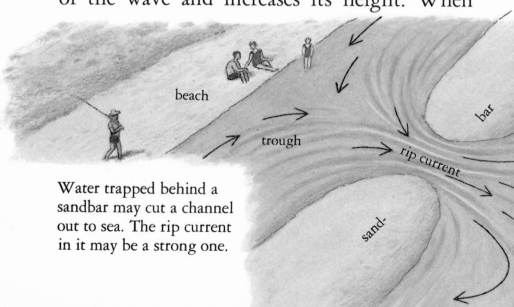

beach

trough

bar

rip current

sand-

Water trapped behind a sandbar may cut a channel out to sea. The rip current in it may be a strong one.

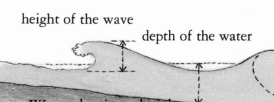

height of the wave

depth of the water

Wave orbit is tilted as
wave approaches the beach.

Waves begin to break
when their height is more than
0.7 times the depth of the water.

the height of a shallow-water wave gets to be
about three quarters the depth of the water,
the wave becomes unstable and soon breaks.

On the open sea, the wave particles move
in almost perfect circles. Close to shore, the
drag changes the orbit into an ellipse. The
ellipse becomes longer as the wave tilts toward
the beach.

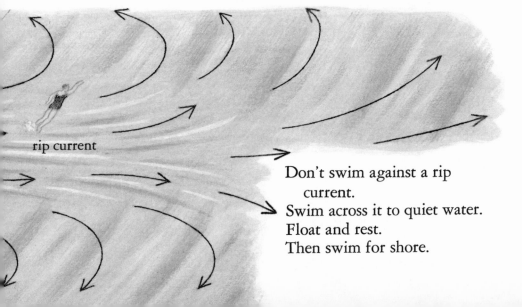

rip current

Don't swim against a rip
current.
Swim across it to quiet water.
Float and rest.
Then swim for shore.

By this time the wave has moved into water that is only one and a half times as deep as the wave is high. Now there is not enough water moving seaward in front of the wave to fill the complete crest. Without the support of water beneath, the wave breaks. The crest spills over or crashes with a roar.

Where waves break, the surf begins. This point may be only a few yards from shore. But if the bottom slopes gently and the waves are large, the surf may form a mile out to sea.

Waves breaking on the shore bring with

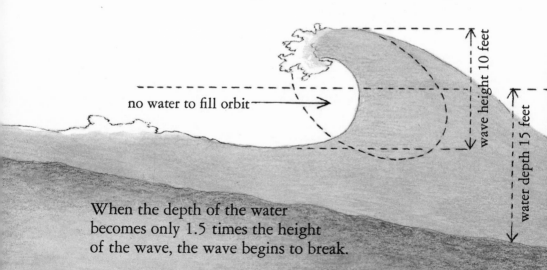

no water to fill orbit

wave height 10 feet

water depth 15 feet

When the depth of the water becomes only 1.5 times the height of the wave, the wave begins to break.

them the energy of winds that may have been blowing a week before—thousands of miles away. Just when, where, and how a wave will break have no single answer. The usual wave, however, keeps its form till the second it plunges.

Sometimes the beach slope is very shallow, perhaps with rocky patches on the bottom that increase the drag. Then waves are less likely to break. They spill over slowly, taking much more time to roll up on the shore. Such spilling waves have made some beaches of Hawaii, South Africa, and Australia famous for surf riding. There waves carry a skilled rider half a mile or more. Plunging waves break in a much shorter distance and, when large, are far more dangerous to surfers or swimmers.

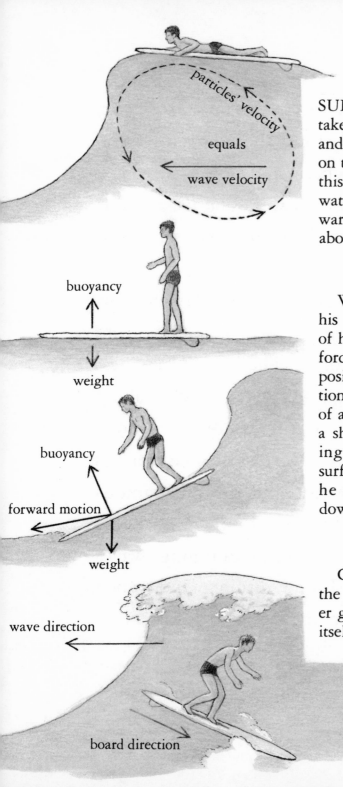

SURFING is a sport that takes advantage of the form and motion of a wave that is on the verge of breaking. At this point the speed of the water particles and the forward speed of the wave are about equal.

When a surfer floats on his board the buoyant force of his floating board and the force of his weight are opposite one another. No motion results. But on the front of a wave these forces are at a sharper angle with resulting forward motion. The surfer keeps moving because he is continually sliding downhill.

Going at an angle down the face of the wave the surfer goes faster than the wave itself. All this takes skill.

The surf on most beaches is constantly shifting. Tides raise and lower the water level several feet or more, changing the surf. The wind changes it too. A number of other conditions affect the way waves break and how their energy is released on the shore.

People have called the beach the battle-ground between land and sea. It often is. The pounding of waves and surf wears down the land in some places, and in others the sea slowly builds up beaches, marshes, and dunes. This work of tearing down and building up land has been going on for millions upon

waves on a rocky shore

millions of years. It is of the greatest importance in shaping the surface of the earth.

The breaking of waves finally releases energy from the sun which heats the air, which makes the wind, which raises the waves, which pound the beach. Each wave that breaks moves sand back and forth. In winter, when winds are stronger and waves steeper, more sand is removed from the shore. In summer, the low, long waves bring sand back again.

Sand may move toward one side or another of a beach with a steady wind or current. A single storm shifts great amounts of sand, but slow movement, year after year, is what changes the shore, as old maps often

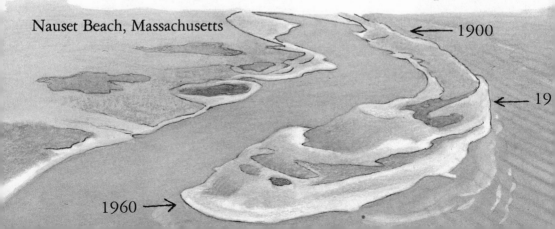

Nauset Beach, Massachusetts

1900

19

1960

Jetties are walls to prevent sand blocking the mouth of a river.

sandy beach

show. Spits of land are formed by moving beach sand. Sometimes bays are cut off from the sea.

Man's use of the shore is complicated by shifting sand. Harbors are built, and keeping them open for ships to enter is essential. The mouths of rivers must be kept open, too. Also, since millions of people live along our shores and many millions more come to them for vacations, protecting beaches as part of our national heritage is only wise.

So the movement of sand along the shore-
line becomes a matter of dollars and cents.
The harbor at Salina Cruz, Mexico, like many
others, has to be constantly dredged. About
a million tons of sand a year move into the
harbor of Madras, India. When a breakwater
was finished at Santa Monica, California, sand
began to pile against it at the rate of about
half a million tons a year. To the north, at
Santa Barbara, almost a thousand tons of sand

Dredges keep harbors
open by removing sand.

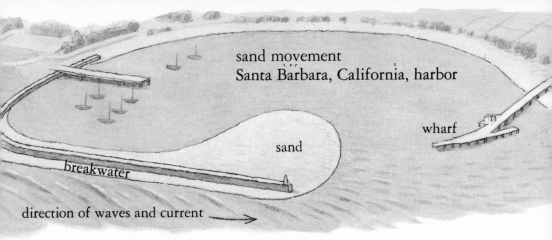

sand movement
Santa Barbara, California, harbor

wharf

sand

breakwater

direction of waves and current ⟶

a day are pushed by waves and currents around the ends of the breakwater.

There seems to be no easy method of keeping sand in place. Sometimes rows of rocks or posts, called groins, are set up across the beach to stop the movement of sand. For a while these devices are effective, but groins apparently are not always the final answer.

Groins may protect a beach for years.

Where sand has piled up at one end of a beach it is often pumped back to fill in the area that was "robbed." Then the process starts all over again.

The movement of sand is usually so slow that from day to day nothing is noticed. Only as months go by do we begin to see the great amount of material that has shifted. But

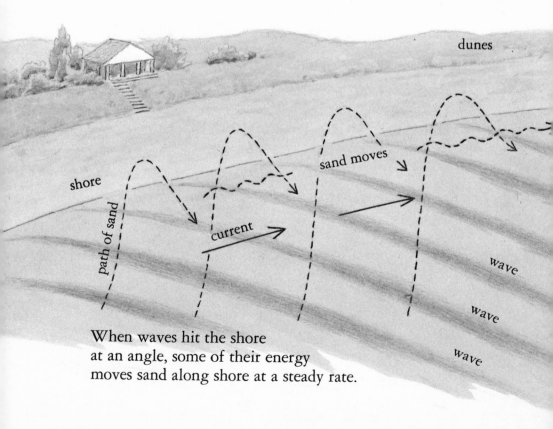

When waves hit the shore at an angle, some of their energy moves sand along shore at a steady rate.

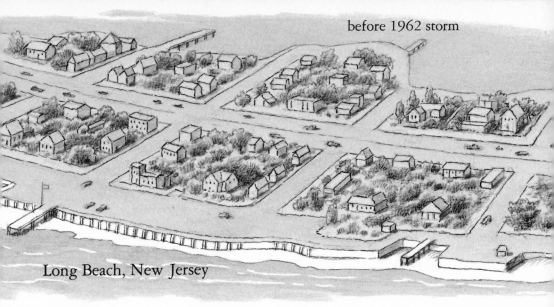

before 1962 storm

Long Beach, New Jersey

where a storm hits the coast and waves increase in size from 2 to 10 times, beaches change before our eyes. Damage to houses, piers, and to the beach itself runs into millions of dollars.

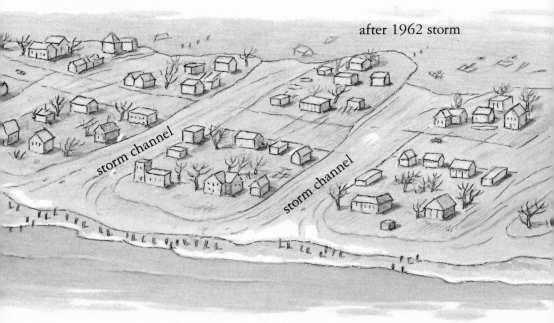

after 1962 storm

storm channel

storm channel

breakwater after storm damage

The power of breaking waves is seen most clearly when they strike walls, cliffs, or break-waters. Waves that meet a wall before they break are reflected back to sea with little loss of energy. But when the wave breaks, the tumbling crest hurls tons of water against an obstacle. Rocks weighing many tons are moved. Whole lighthouses have been torn down.

Engineers tell the story of the breakwater, at Wick Bay in Scotland, which was capped by huge stone blocks cemented and tied together with heavy iron rods. The mass weighing 1350 tons was moved several feet in a storm. The breakwater was repaired and strengthened, but five years later the new cap, now weighing 2600 tons, was shifted three feet in another storm.

Heavy four-legged concrete structures are used to build and protect modern breakwaters.

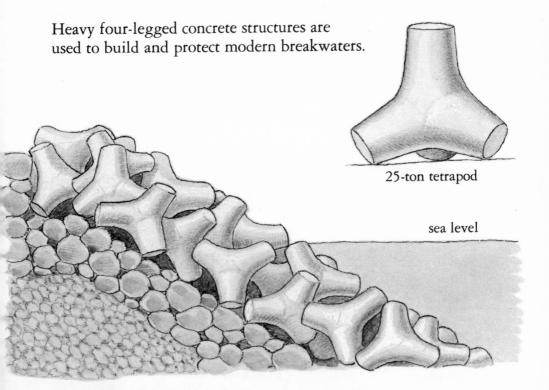

25-ton tetrapod

sea level

Rocks weighing several tons have been tossed like pebbles. At the Tillamook lighthouse on the Oregon coast, waves hurled a rock weighing 135 pounds higher than the 140-foot lighthouse. It dropped through the roof of a building that was nearly 100 feet above sea level.

Measurements in tanks and the study of damage done suggest that breaking waves often exert a push of 1000 to 2000 pounds on each square foot. During storms the pressure may be twice as high, if not more. Moreover,

Tillamook Rock Lighthouse

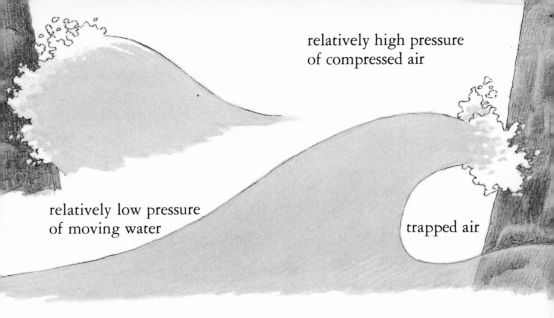

relatively high pressure
of compressed air

relatively low pressure
of moving water

trapped air

when the wave breaks so that a pocket of air is caught under the crest, the air is compressed. For a fraction of a second the compressed air may exert a pressure of over 10,000 pounds, or five tons, per square foot.

The steady push of winds causes ocean waves. But a tsunami (pronounced soo-no-me), or tidal wave, is caused by some other sudden action. This action quickly raises or lowers an area of ocean bottom. Water, rushing in or out, starts the tsunami waves.

The ocean gets the up or down push that starts a tidal wave in three ways. A large landslide in the soft deposits of mud and sand along a steep continental shelf may occur. If millions of tons of sediments slip down, the nearby water may be given a tremendous push.

The explosion of a volcano may send tsunami waves moving across the Pacific.

Earthquakes underneath the sea do the same

thing—sometimes on a larger scale. If an area of the ocean floor moves up or drops down rapidly, the water is moved too. Most tsunamis,

submarine landslide

volcano erupts

or tidal waves, are caused by earthquakes, also known as seismic disturbances.

The push given to the water by an earthquake is not great when you think of the ocean as a whole. But the surface in one area

need move up and down only a few feet to start a tidal wave. From a ship in deep water, this wave may not be noticed at all.

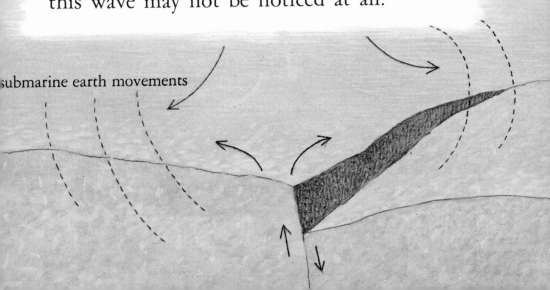

submarine earth movements

depth 2 miles

waves 2 feet high
speed 300 to 600 miles an hour
depending on depth

depth 1 m

Tsunami waves are very different from wind waves. They are quite low and perhaps as much as 100 or 150 miles long. Because they are so long, their period is long too. It lasts about 10 to 15 minutes instead of a few seconds as does that of ordinary waves.

In the deep waters of the Pacific a tsunami

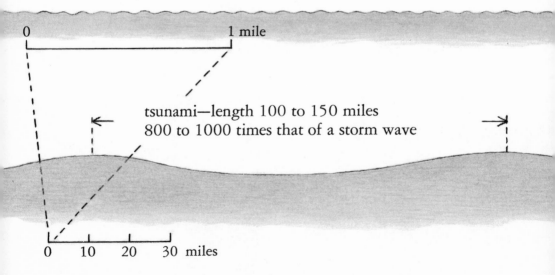

storm wave—length 500 to 700 feet

0   1 mile

tsunami—length 100 to 150 miles
800 to 1000 times that of a storm wave

0   10   20   30   miles

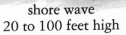

depth 1/10 mile

shore wave
20 to 100 feet high

Wave decreases in speed
and builds up in height.

wave may travel nearly 600 miles an hour. The long waves traveling at jet speed are hard to see. But as they come close to shore, their speed slows down and the height builds up. Then the tsunami changes into a wave that may rise 10 to 100 feet high.

The force of the earthquake, its distance, the slope of the sea bottom, and other factors affect the size and number of tsunami waves that reach the shore. Only a few may come, or there may be as many as two dozen. Tidal waves can destroy everything in one area, yet do very little damage a short distance away.

If tsunami waves approach during the day, the first small waves may not be noticed by

people at the beach. What does attract atten-
tion, more often, is the way the sea with-
draws. It may roll back like a very low tide
and expose more of the bottom than people
have ever seen before, grounding small boats
and leaving fish flapping on the sand.

This retreat of the sea is really the trough
of a long-period wave reaching the shore. The
water may recede for ten minutes or more,
and this retreat, which seems like a very low

A sudden withdrawal of the sea
may be the start of a tsunami.

tide, is the origin of the name "tidal wave." The Japanese name, tsunami, means a wave seen on shore, but not on the open sea.

The receding water is a warning of the tsunami to come. On some coasts it may arrive as a great churning wave. More often it is like a fast-rising tide that is in full flood about fifteen minutes after the lowest water. Each of the several waves can destroy everything in its path, as it advances and retreats.

Since the beginning of history, stories of these great tidal waves appear over and over again. Most of the damage has been along the borders of the Pacific and its many islands. But one of the oldest tsunamis took place on the island of Crete about 1400 B.C. Records tell of more than 300 major tidal waves in which thousands upon thousands of people perished.

Until recently tidal waves came without warning. Cities were destroyed and most of their people killed overnight. Tsunamis have caused havoc from Chile, north through Peru, and up the California coast into Alaska. Japan has been hit many times and so has Hawaii and other Pacific islands.

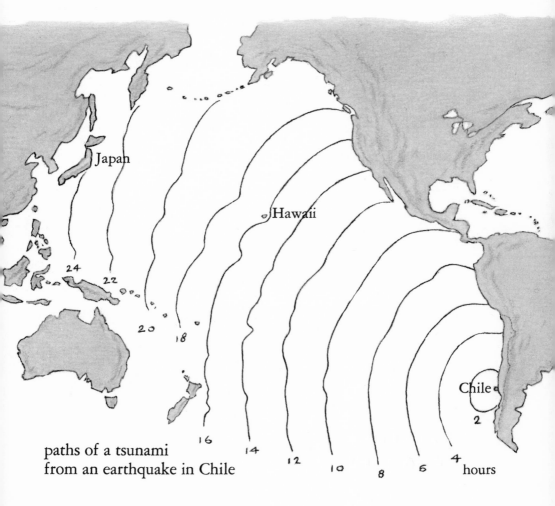

paths of a tsunami
from an earthquake in Chile

The explosion of the volcano Krakatoa in 1883 started a tidal wave near the East Indies that killed over 36,000 people. After the great Lisbon earthquake, in 1755, giant waves flooded towns on the coast of Spain and Portugal. In 1896 a tsunami in Japan destroyed 10,000 homes and about 30,000 people.

In 1946 an underwater earthquake in the Aleutian Islands sent tidal waves tearing through the Pacific. Waves over 100 feet high hit the nearby Alaskan coast. A two-story lighthouse at Unimak Island, over 30 feet above sea level, was completely destroyed; so was a radio tower 100 feet above the water.

The waves rushed south and westward, reaching the Hawaiian Islands in five hours. Those that struck Hilo were as high as 50 feet. The entire lower part of the town was demolished. But the captain of a ship, outside the port, felt nothing as the waves passed. Moments later he watched with amazement the destruction on land. Many small villages on low Pacific islands were also ruined. Some were 4000 to 5000 miles away from the site of the earthquake.

damage at Hilo

Again in 1964, on the Alaskan coast, a severe earthquake sent a tsunami speeding through the sea. Hardest hit were towns so close they had practically no warning. At the Valdez dock a 10,000-ton ship touched bottom three times as the water rose and fell. It managed to get up steam and escape, though the pier and nearby buildings vanished. A 30-foot surge struck Kodiak destroying the large fishing fleet. At Seward, docks were swept away. Four hours later a 9-foot wave bore in on Crescent City, California, and an hour or so afterward the tsunami reached Hawaii. In all, 115 people were killed. Damage, most of it near the earthquake center, passed the half-billion dollar mark.

damage in Alaska

Among the many tragic stories of tsunami is one with a touch of humor. About a hundred years ago an American sidewheel battleship lay at anchor in the harbor of Arica in northern Chile. An undersea earthquake sent a wall of water over the city. It lifted the battleship from its moorings, carried it over the trees and buildings, and set it down gently more than a mile inland.

The captain sent word to the Navy asking for help. While awaiting a reply he had his men plant gardens to increase the food supply. To carry out his inspections, he climbed down the ship's ladder to a burro instead of into his boat. Months went by before the landlocked ship was sold and the crew returned home on another ship.

After the 1946 tsunami, the United States government began to work on a warning system to alert Hawaii if a tidal wave approached. The job fell to the Coast and Geodetic Survey. Within two years a system was developed. Tsunamis cannot be prevented, but people can move to safety if they are warned several hours in advance.

The warning system has a long name—the Seismic Sea-wave Warning System. It is written as SSWWS, which nobody can pronounce as a word. The system goes into action whenever a seismic disturbance—an earthquake—occurs under or near the sea. First, the location of the disturbance and its strength are established by measuring the earthquake waves that spread rapidly through the earth's crust.

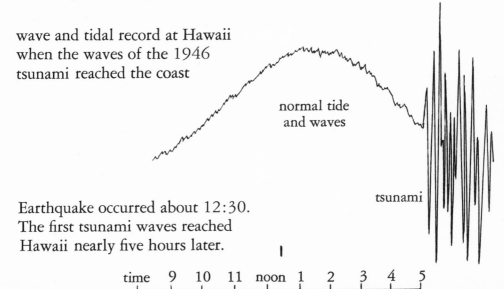

wave and tidal record at Hawaii when the waves of the 1946 tsunami reached the coast

normal tide and waves

tsunami

Earthquake occurred about 12:30. The first tsunami waves reached Hawaii nearly five hours later.

time   9   10   11   noon   1   2   3   4   5

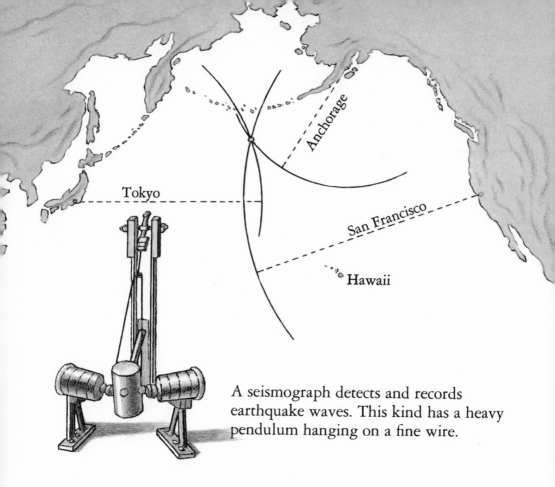

Tokyo

Anchorage

San Francisco

Hawaii

A seismograph detects and records earthquake waves. This kind has a heavy pendulum hanging on a fine wire.

At many places delicate instruments called seismographs have been set up to detect and measure earthquakes. From the record made by a moving needle, scientists at each station measure the direction and distance of the earthquake along a curve, which they draw on a map. As soon as two or three reports are in, the curves around each of the stations are plotted. The earthquake is located at the place where the curves cross. The size of the vibrations on the seismograph record tell how severe the earthquake was.

When reports indicate that the earthquake

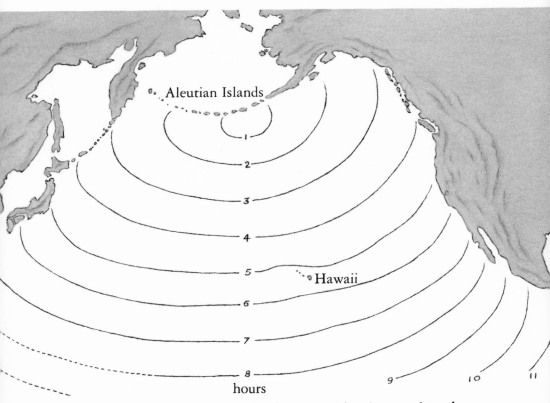

tsunami paths from an Aleutian earthquake

may cause a tidal wave, the central station at Hawaii radios a tsunami alert to all stations that are part of the SSWWS program. More information may come in from special tide gauges that have been set up at many places in the Pacific. Observers, especially those near the earthquake source, watch for any sign of a tidal wave. The first sighting is final proof that a tidal wave is moving across the Pacific.

At Hawaii, new bulletins go out, giving a firm warning and estimating the time that the tidal wave should arrive at key places. Thus all the SSWWS stations on Pacific is-lands and shores are alerted. Word is passed to the police and harbor authorities. The warning is quickly relayed to all people living along the shore. Usually they have advance notice of several hours.

Since the SSWWS warning program was started in 1948, a number of tidal waves have occurred. In 1952 the system had its first test. A tidal wave from the north Pacific moved south. Hawaii was warned. The waves caused much damage, but no lives were lost. Since then, tidal waves have killed far fewer people.

The SSWWS program has now been extended. Warnings reach nearly every part of the Pacific, where local people spread the alarm as far and as fast as possible.

For many years people thought of the daily tides as long, low waves flowing around the earth. Studies have shown that this is not so and that tides differ greatly from wind-driven waves. Caused by the pull of moon and sun, tides are a kind of standing wave in each of the ocean's many overlapping basins. When the tide is high on one side of a basin, it is low on the other, and, at the center, there is no tide at all.

Engineers have worked out ways to use the energy of tides to make electricity. Someday they may do the same with ordinary waves. Meanwhile, the study of waves continues.

Bay of Fundy

high tide

low tide

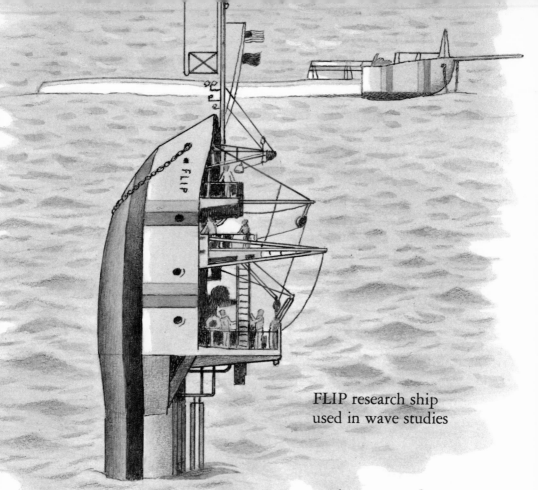

FLIP research ship
used in wave studies

FLIP, the research ship that can be turned up on end to become a floating instrument platform, has been used to investigate how waves spread. Although much remains to be learned, scientists are sure of one thing. Waves will be here to see and enjoy as long as seas exist.

INDEX

Date Due

APR 28 '70	FEB. 1 4 1993			
MY 1 '72	NOV. 2 2 1994			
MR 31 '74	DEC. 1 0 1994			
FEB 15 '77	NOV 2 7 2001			
FEB 17 '77				
MAY 19 '77				
MAY 18 '79				
MAY 11 '85				
FEB 2 2 1990				

PRINTED IN U.S.A. CAT. NO. 23231

J
551.4
Z   58486

AUTHOR
Zim, Herbert Spencer
TITLE
Waves.

58486

J
551.4
Z

Zim, Herbert Spencer
Waves.

COLLEGE LIBRARY
ST. MARY OF THE SPRINGS
COLUMBUS, OHIO